IN THE KEY OF

BELIEVE

MATTHEW DOUGLAS PINARD

MATTHEWDOUGLASPINARD.COM

MW01247734

Copyright © 2023 Matthew Douglas Pinard

All Rights Reserved. No part of this book publication may be reproduced or transmitted in any form or by any means, mechanical or electronic, including photocopying, scanning, and recording, or by any information storage and retrieval system, or other -- without prior permission in writing from the author or publisher. Disclaimers: The Publisher and the Author make no representation or warranties concerning the accuracy or completeness of the contents of this work and specifically disclaim all warranties for a particular purpose. No warranty may be created or extended through sales or promotional materials. The advice and strategies contained herein may not be suitable for every situation. This work is sold with the understanding that the Author and Publisher are not engaged in rendering legal, technological, or other professional services. If professional assistance is required, the services of a competent professional should be sought. Neither the Publisher nor the Author shall be liable for damages arising therefrom. The fact that an organization or website is referred to in this work as a citation and/or potential source of further information does not mean that the Author or the Publisher endorses the information, the organization, or website it may provide, or recommendations it may make. Further, readers should be aware that the websites listed in this work may have changed or disappeared between the time that this work was written and when it is read. Details of the cases and stories in this book have been changed to preserve privacy.

Printed in the United States of America
Published by: Writer's Publishing House
Prescott, AZ 86301

Cover and Interior Design by Creative Artistic Excellence Marketing
Project Management and Book Launch by Creative Artistic Excellence Marketing
https://lizzymcnett.com

Paperback ISBN: 978-1-64873-409-0
Hardcover ISBN: 978-1-64873-410-6

Forward

I am honored to write the Foreword for Matthew's latest book – *In The Key of Believe*. If you have been waiting as I have, our wait is over, and since I got a sneak peek preview to write this Foreword, let me say, "You won't be disappointed."

Matthew wears many hats in the healing field, and he wears them all with grace and understanding of a subject seen as taboo by many in our changing world. Not everyone is ready for Matthew; he is a dynamic personality and author and tells it like it is.

I am always happy to see his new cloud pictures; he takes a lot of them! Follow along with the sequences, and you will find many answers. We share the same sky space, and it is always fun to get his pictures and then run out and see if I can get the same image before it changes.

God, Source, whatever you call your higher power, speaks to us in many different ways. Matthew has always been a cloud reader and sees his answers in the clouds. He is seeing the initials and hearts of those he has brought healing to in such a demonstrative way. In fact – Matthew performed an after-the-fact healing for me last month. I had an ablation surgery for aFib. The surgeon goes in and disrupts the track the aFib is running on in my heart and creates a new path for it. Thus hoping to eliminate the occurrences of aFib as it no longer has the same track to run on.

Matthew knew nothing of my surgery when I called him to pray for post-operative healing. Within minutes of his praying, he sent me the following picture. It was perfect! He saw the "J," and I explained the rest.

From the picture, you can see two tracks – the bottom track is the new track created when the top track was burned with a spark of electricity (the flash of sun or light) to turn off one track, thus making the new track. The blue orb above the spark belongs to my Arcturian star being family watching over me and the operation. The "J" at the bottom of the picture told Matthew this was my cloud and his answer.

I shared what I understood his cloud picture to represent. Have you studied the clouds around you lately? I, too, believe the clouds are the playground for the angels who love to send us messages daily – all that is required is to look up.

Matthew is a healer and mystic within his church. He is blessed with an amazing gift of healing that he gladly shares with all who ask him. His talents have expanded from being a healer, and his psychic abilities allow him to reach out beyond time and space to find clues to find missing persons.

The stories you are about to read are a small sampling of Matthew's ability to effect healing in others while empowering them to find the key of believe in their healing powers. Matthew shares his tools and stories in various venues (YouTube, podcasts, etc.) Listen in some time; you won't be disappointed. And the next time you look up in the sky and see a cloud, smile – know you have not been forgotten.

Jeri K. Tory Conklin, Author – "When Spirits Speak" series

MATTHEW DOUGLAS PINARD

hello!

6

Catholic Mystic and award-winning author and screenwriter Matthew Douglas Pinard is the author of seven books on angels, the afterlife, psychic clairvoyance, prophecy, and miraculous healing.
Matthew will help you communicate with loved ones who have passed and are angel spirit guides to protect and help us navigate this world.

The author explains his encounter with "The Woman Clothed with the Sun." He became a witness to an amazing precious blood miracle the Vatican is now investigating. It preceded three amazing healing miracles of degenerative diseases among friends and family.

Matthew's photographs will send chills down your spine, proving life exists in other dimensions outside the physical realm. This is a once-in-a-lifetime chance to unlock the deepest mysteries of your own life, bringing this world closer to peace, light, healing, and hope.

COPYRIGHT © 2023 MATTHEW DOUGLAS PINARD

Contents

TOP
ANGEL

THE INITIAL CHAPTER OF *"IN THE KEY OF BELIEVE"*
IS DEDICATED TO THE TOP ANGEL VISITATIONS OF 2022.

Top Angel

AN INCREDIBLE IMAGE OF A FEMALE ANGEL SHOOTING UP INTO THE SKIES ABOVE ARIZONA LIKE A JET ON DECEMBER 5TH, 2022 AS I FINISHED *IN THE KEY OF BELIEVE.*

As the world teeters on the brink of Armageddon, with World War III looming in the background, the 'plandemics' constructed by the Nazi (kirstallnacht) regime, not to mention the mandates that tried to force vaccinations upon the population around the world, our skies have been filled with promising messages of a brighter future ahead.

On December 5th 2022, an angel appeared in the sky as I finished the book. She represents the birth of a new society, not shrouded in agenda meant to keep the population in slavery, nor a world order who controls the financial system of everyone on the planet, but peace throughout the human race.

I personally photographed the cloud formation in hopes of inspiring this world to become one with the other kingdom and change the course of human history before it's too late.

'S' FOR HER
BRAIN

THIS WAS THE FIRST 'S' AFTER PRAYING FOR A WOMAN WITH STAGE IV BRAIN CANCER WHOSE FIRST NAME BEGINS WITH AN S.

Sweety

In the Spring of 2022, my publisher Lizzy McNett told me her client's wife had been diagnosed with Stage IV brain cancer. Lizzy asked for my prayers, and since she published the previous Angel Healing books, she was acutely aware of the power of prayers for healing.

After learning of the story, I knew her name started with an S., but the amazing part of this story is her client lives in India. I nevertheless started the next day with a Rosary for her miraculous recovery and struggle against an insidious disease.

Almost immediately amazing signs and wonders began to appear in the skies, and I have continuously gotten almost one hundred "S's" in the skies above Arizona, Colorado, and even on a vacation to Hawaii. It was incredible.

The angel response was overwhelming and occurred consistently over the next six months. After speaking with Lizzy recently for an update, unbelievably it appears as if her client's wife will make a full recovery from this late-stage cancer.

Can I say for certain it was the angels over modern medicine responsible for this incredible turn of events? No, but I can say there is no doubt in my mind their response played a huge role in her recovery. I will also say almost every time I took one of the photos you will see below, I received a huge "chill" from the top of my head down the bottom of my spine.

In keeping with the theme the key of believe was an incredible experience for me praying for someone I have never met and lives on the other side of the world. As I mentioned in previous books, there are two keys to the other kingdom. One is "be love" and the other is "believe."

But as in praying for this woman, I believed she could be healed. As just the feeling I received when praying for my father's lungs. My goal for this book is to highlight that everyone can engage the other kingdom and heal themselves and others even in the face of unsurmountable odds.

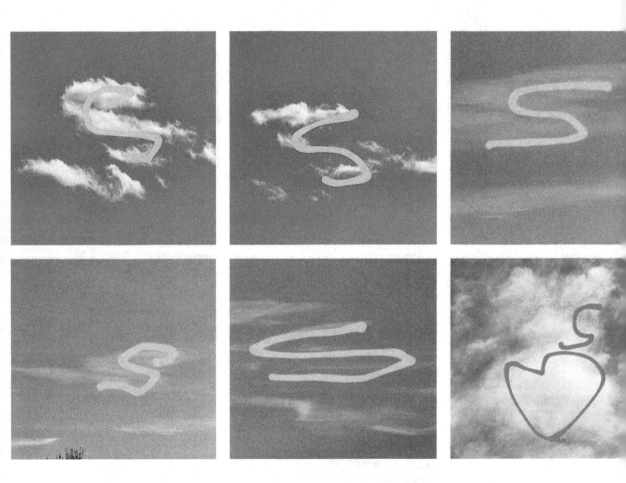

More amazing "S's" appear in the skies above Arizona during 2022 for a woman battling Stage IV brain cancer. More hearts also appeared in these frames.

ALL DOGS GOTO
HEAVEN

IN THE FALL OF 2022 AFTER PUTTING DOWN OUR TWO DOGS *REESE*
AND CLEETUS, I VISITED THE YAVAPAI HUMANE SOCIETY ASKING FOR
A SIGN FROM THE ANGELS IF I WAS GOING TO MEET MY NEW PUPPY
TODAY.

Dogs

One of the most heart wrenching experiences anyone has to participate in is putting a pet to sleep. In most cases, we often feel more pain from losing a pet than some humans. Reese and Cleetus were part of our family for many years. Their loss was devastating for myself and wife.

I know my feeling might seem wrong, but I am being honest. Pets are true gifts from the other kingdom, as they love unconditionally and without judgment.

What was amazing about both Reese and Cleetus was that as soon as we put them down, they both immediately appeared in the skies riding high as angels. If you've ever had any doubts about whether a dog has a soul and where that soul goes, take a close look at the amazing photos below.

Photo: In the fall of 2022 after putting down our two dogs
Reese and Cleetus,

Reese and Cleetus in life and afterlife. We carved a pumpkin as Cleetus' face and the same night he appeared in the skies above central Arizona in the fall of 2022. Both dogs loved us unconditionally and were always there for us even in difficult times.

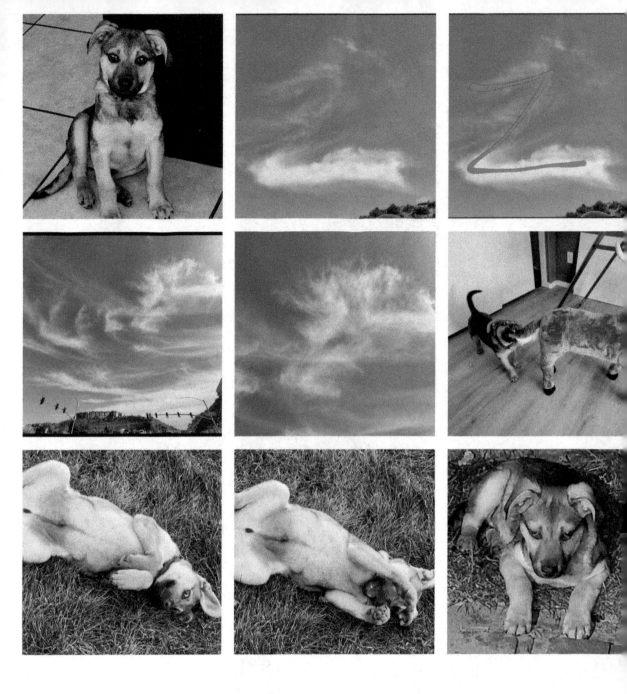

Photo: Upon walking into the humane society there was a huge "Z" above the building. A little German Shepard and Husky mix puppy grabbed my attention. His name happened to be "Zarkov." We renamed him Gabriel Zarkov. The "Z" was all the sign that I needed I had met my new full of love dog.

'Key of Believe'

Seeing the power of animal spirits firsthand reminds me that all organisms are gifts from God.

Imagine imparting that knowledge to a world that continues to have senseless wars, racism, and school shootings. If only this world could grasp the concept of the key of believe.

AN 'E' FOR
HER SPINE

PHOTO: AN INCREDIBLE IMAGE OF A "CURVED" SPINE, DEMONIC
FACE, AND AN "E" FORMING ALONG WITH AN F-1 TORNADO ABOVE
PRESCOTT VALLEY, ARIZONA IN EARLY OCTOBER 2022.

Scoliosis

IN MID-2022, A WOMAN WHOSE NAME BEGAN WITH 'K' ASKED ME TO PRAY FOR HER DAUGHTER. IN A SHORT TIME, "E'S" BEGAN SHOWING UP EVERYWHERE. THE DAUGHTER'S NAME STARTED WITH AN E AND WAS RECENTLY DIAGNOSED WITH SCOLIOSIS.

After viewing imaging, the spinal column was still curved fairly severely, even after numerous surgical and chiropractic treatments. I began daily prayers for her to be fully healed. What happened next is beyond words....

Over one hundred enormous Es appeared in the skies above central Arizona. In early October 2022, I was at home working on the skies. Suddenly they turned an ominous gray, the next few minutes were remarkable.

The image appeared to show a "curved" spine in the middle of the sky, with a huge "E" towards the bottom of the spine. I said prayers that morning for this young woman to be cured of her scoliosis when that same demonic-looking cloud manifested above my roof. It appears to show a demonic-looking face to the right of the curved spine above the "E."

What's interesting is that some cultures believe scoliosis is actually a result of demonic attack or possession. As this curved spine, demonic face and "E" appeared, a huge storm front rolled into our neighborhood, bringing thrashing rains and high winds. It was later confirmed that an F-1 tornado actually touched down. It was as if I witnessed the higher angels of light drive the "disease" out of this spine and the demon along with it.

As of this date, we don't have evidence of a full recovery from her scoliosis, but her mother told me, it will be a miracle if it does not get any worse. I, for one, definitely believe a miracle can still occur for this young lady, and when it does it will be in the "key to belief."

Photo: Incredible images of angels bringing huge healing "E's" to earth to help
a young lady whose first initial is "E" as she battles severe scoliosis in 2022.
You can see multiple "E's" in some of these shots.

A YELLOW BIRD

A PIGGY BANK, AND THEN RAIN

PHOTO: A PHOTO OF MICHELLE'S SON MATTHEW WHO AFTER A DIFFICULT STRUGGLE ON THIS SIDE IS NOW A GREAT SPIRITUAL WARRIOR WITH JESUS ON THE OTHER SIDE.

Heartbreaking

THE NEXT TWO STORIES ARE BOTH HEARTBREAKING, BUT BEAUTIFULLY AMAZINGLY TO SHOW PROOF OF LIFE BEYOND THIS REALM.

In early 2021, a woman contacted me named Michelle Bailey Rouse, heard of my books and desperately wanted me to contact her son Matthew, who died suddenly in 2017.
To make matters worse, Michelle's husband Darin died suddenly in April 2022 after an illness. The story began to get interesting. Michelle wanted to know if her husband successfully passed on. A completely understandable request.

It seemed her son's death was reported suspicious; a 'suicide pact' between a married couple. Matthew was married to a woman named Nicole, who claimed he died after swallowing sleeping pills after agreeing to a suicide pact.

After numerous prayers to bring Matthew's spirit to us, I was shown an image of a hypodermic needle, which was interesting because Matthew's autopsy showed an unexplained puncture wound on his skin. I explained to Michelle that the police should have investigated this as a homicide since his wife took out a life insurance policy shortly before the suicide pact.

As of this writing, Nicole was convicted of a felony in assisting a suicide exactly five years after his death. All claims to death benefits have been denied.

Once we contacted Matthew's spirit, I told Michelle some things only the two of them would know. First, a black cat with yellow eyes appeared. She confirmed it was a pet named Gracie. The interesting part is Michelle did not get the cat until after Matthew's death; verifying vision from the other side.

We also learned Matthew felt he had access to a great spiritual power but couldn't connect to it in this realm. Michelle confirmed they discussed the struggles he'd faced in life.

The image of his situation became clear, so I informed Michelle that he is a strong spiritual warrior with a flaming sword, like an Angel, who is battling demons in the afterlife. My visions calmed her soul, so she could move forward knowing her loved ones were fulfilling their destiny.

As with all my client sessions, we ask the heavens to give us signs. The following images show amazing "Ms" in the skies and an incredible face in the clouds, which appears to be the face of Jesus superimposed onto the face of Matthew.

Following the incredible interactions with Matthew, I had similar experiences contacting Michelle's husband Darin. After multiple "Ds" appeared in the skies above Arizona, I was given an incredibly clairvoyant prophetic set of images from Darin.

The images were a piggy bank, a yellow bird on a cell phone, and an image of rain falling. After finding out the piggy bank belonged to Darin's favorite grandson Coy, who was undergoing some dental procedures the next day. However, three days later, after giving these images to Michelle, she sent me a text.

"I got my yellow bird from Darin as a surprise on my phone today! Darin's sister and her husband are on a month-long vacation. Today they were at the beach in North Carolina and a yellow Spirit Airlines plane flew overheard across the screen as it was also raining at my house."

Photo: An image of Darin Rouse, husband of Michelle Bailey Rouse prior to his passing in 2022 after a battle with an illness. Darin gave us amazing messages from the other side proving he could see days into the future.

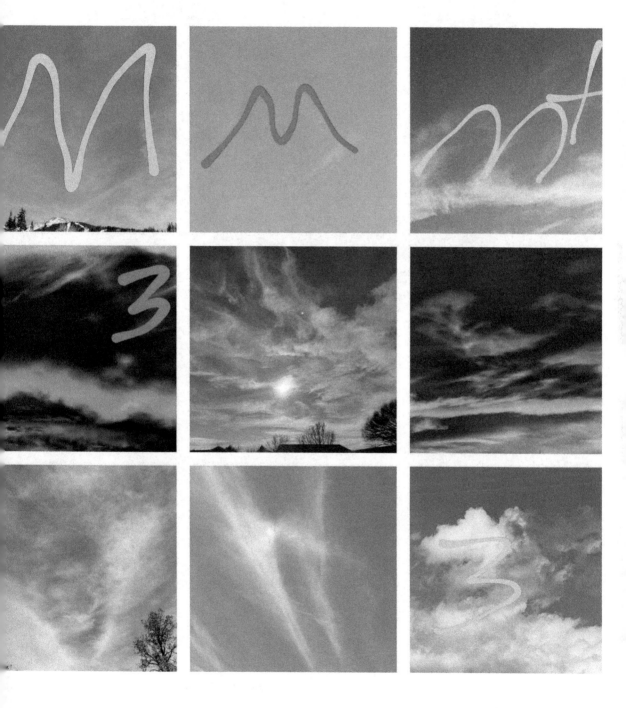

Photo: This incredible photo shows a male face looking down to the right of the frame.This was taken the evening before incredibly prophetic messages were given to us by Darin Rouse for his wife Michelle Bailey Rouse.

Key of Believe

I admit assisting Michelle Bailey Rouse with the connection of her passed-on loved ones has been one of the most rewarding experiences in my life.

I know her heart is heavy, but seeing and hearing these messages from the other side is a comfort to all of us that there is life after death -- it is a new beginning.

TRACEY'S
WOLF

PHOTO: TRACEY B., AN OLD FRIEND, WHO ALSO SEEMS TO HAVE BEEN CURED OF HER LUPUS WOLF-LIKE SYMPTOMS IN 2022. LUPUS IS AN AUTO-IMMUNE DISORDER IN WHICH THE BODY'S IMMUNE SYSTEM ATTACKS THE BODY CAUSING INFLAMMATION AND PAIN.

Full Remission

MULTIPLE HEARTS AND THE INITIALS "T.B." APPEAR IN THE SKIES ABOVE CENTRAL ARIZONA IN 2022 WHILE PRAYING FOR A WOMAN NAMED TRACEY B. WITH LUPUS. YOU CAN CLEARLY SEE A HEART ABOVE A CHURCH AND A HUGE RAINBOW AND TWO BEAUTIFUL SUNSETS.

In the 1990s, my brother dated a woman named Tracey B. who reached out in 2022. We had not spoken or seen each other since then. She was battling the same wolf as J.C. discussed in this book (page 118) -- immune disorder lupus. During the conversation, I mentioned some of the other miraculous healings I've witnessed or instigated upon request.

Almost immediately, we received an amazing response from the other kingdom. Many large "Ts" and "Bs" appeared in the skies shown in the images. In addition to rainbows, hearts, and huge angels with gorgeous sunsets.

Tracey made her next medical appointment, the tests showed full remission. The wolf was tamed.

'Key of Believe'

The miracles I have witnessed taught me how the process of my methods work. There is no doubt Tracey B's Lupus being in remission is due to her trust, not to mention, both of us fully believing the angels from the other kingdom can deliver countless miracles all in the key of believe.

THE DEATH OF
LUIGI

THE NEXT STORY, QUITE FRANKLY, IS ONE OF THE MOST AMAZING
EXPERIENCES OF MY LIFE. IN EARLY 2021, A FRIEND ASKED ME TO
PRAY FOR HER GOOD FRIEND – HER NAME BEGINS WITH 'D'.

Daily Prayers

AMAZING HEARTS AND "D'S" APPEAR ABOVE CENTRAL ARIZONA IN 2022 AFTER PRAYERS FOR A MAN NAMED "D" WITH A VERY SERIOUS HEART TUMOR. "D" WAS GIVEN ONLY A FEW MONTHS TO A YEAR AND A HALF TO LIVE AFTER HIS DIAGNOSIS

We used the 'D' for deadly rare diseases. The diagnosis was for the heart condition called synovial sarcoma, in effect, terminal heart cancer. His doctors said six to eighteen months to live. The testing showed a tumor the size of a Pepsi can – the only options were surgery, radiation, or chemo.

D's heart cancer appeared terminal, but I started daily prayers asking that his cancer simply vanish. The challenging part, one of his close friends, an 'atheist', said nothing could be done, and praying was futile. I simply by-passed the connotation and moved forward with my process. Within a short time, incredibly huge angels, hearts, large "Ds" and even a few hearts showing a smaller mass appeared.

Originally, we were told D started on chemo, but that was all information given. However, early on he quit chemotherapy, thinking it was only going to make him sick and not help his diagnosis.

After a year and a half with no acknowledgment of his condition, we received this message. The friend who asked me to pray from the beginning sent the text.

"Eighteen months ago, I received a diagnosis of synovial sarcoma of the heart and my oncologist estimated my lifespan at six to eighteen months. On Thursday, I had a CT scan and it showed no metastases and no further growth of the remnant tumor in my heart wall, now about the volume of a small apricot. Before my surgery, radiation, and chemotherapy it was approximately the volume of a soda can. For the moment, the tumor is static and I'm actually becoming rather fond of the little guy (his name is Luigi and his pronouns are he/him) … personally, I think Luigi needs to die, but I will settle for him being still and passive."

Photos: Amazing angels with hearts, a cross, a "D" and a rainbow appear in 2022 in central Arizona after prayers for a man with a "terminal" heart cancer diagnosis. In the top two frames to the right, you can even see a smaller-sized "mass" inside the heart-like chamber with the angel.

Photo: Amazing hearts and "D's" appear above central Arizona in 2022 after prayers for a man named "D" with a very serious heart tumor. "D" was given only a few months to a year and a half to live after his diagnosis.

'Key of Believe'

You can obviously see that "D" has a tremendous sense of humor. I also agree with him that Luigi needs to "die" and will be asking the angels to complete the process, all through, of course, the key of believe.

A BLACK
PYRAMID

A MYSTICAL BLACK PYRAMID APPEARS AT SUNRISE TOP LEFT AND
ALSO AT SUNSET MIDDLE TOP ROW ON DECEMBER 6TH, 2022 AFTER A
LUCID VISION. YOU CAN SEE SOMETHING IS HOVERING ABOVE BOTH
PYRAMIDS OR "CARRYING IT" JUST AS MY VISION FORETOLD. THERE
ALSO APPEARS TO BE A BLACK DRAGON BREATHING FIRE IN THE
MIDDLE FRAME AND MORE ANGELS IN THE BOTTOM ROWS. THE
MEANING OF THESE APPARITIONS STILL ELUDES ME.

Cryptic Vision

WHILE FINISHING THE EDITS ON THIS BOOK, SOMETHING ODD HAPPENED, THE DATE WILL STICK IN MY HEAD FOREVER, DECEMBER 5TH, 2022.

An intense lucid vision of thousands of horses dragging a large black pyramid across the sky with ropes. It was hard to grasp being fully awake.

I knew it must be some cryptic vision from the angels, but the meaning perplexed me. However, the revelation did not stop there. On my way to church the next morning, I saw a strange white mist over the mountains near my home, which made it appear like a large black pyramid in the mist. I knew this was not a coincidence.

Later that evening, another black pyramid surrounded by light emanating angels or "horses." I found that in ancient Egypt, the black pyramid was one of five remaining pyramids of the original eleven at Dahshur.

Originally named Amenemhet is Mighty, it earned the name Black Pyramid for its dark, decaying appearance as a rubble mound. The Black Pyramid was the first to house both the deceased pharaoh and his queens. In essence, the Black Pyramid was associated with death and royalty.

The Black Pyramid vision and subsequent apparitions in early December 2022 are fascinating. The world itself seems in a very dark and precarious place, as it teeters on a possible third world war, which would affect the world. I continue to ponder the meaning of this cryptic vision for both the world and my own life.

More amazing images of dark pyramids and angels inside the pyramids appear above my home in central Arizona on December 7th, 2022.

Photo: *As I continued to ponder and pray about the black pyramid vision this incredible image of a mysterious cloud hovering above a black pyramid-shaped mountain near my home in Arizona appeared the morning of our first heavy snowfall on December 12th, 2022.*

Photo: The famous black pyramid of AmenemhEt at DaHshur is said to be the burial ground of ancient Pharaohs and their Queens.

Photo: The Benben stone from the Pyramid of Amenemhat III in Cairo, Egypt. Mount Benben is where the creative god Atum sat. The inscriptions say something like, "Open your face to the king, so that he can see the lord of the horizon and can cross the sky." Legend has it this mysterious stone is not from Earth and has a tie to the Annunaki from Orion who perhaps built the pyramids. The stone is said to have mystical powers.

STORIES

Photo: A sculpture of King Amenemhat III of Egypt.

Photo: On January 4th, 2023 after prayers for world peace at a local Catholic Church in Prescott Valley, Arizona yet another angel appeared holding what looks again like a black pyramid in the mist.

'Key of Believe'

As I pondered all these clear and amazing signs and wonders, I asked yet for another sign if the New Wine was meant to travel to Cairo, Egypt to visit the black pyramid of Amenemhet, and immediately opened the Bible to this passage from Songs of Solomon: "I liken you, my darling, to a mare among Pharaoh's chariot horses."

Remember, my initial vision was of thousands of horses dragging a black pyramid across the sky. On December 8th, 2022, after attending a local Catholic Mass and asking for another sign that I am meant to travel to Cairo, Egypt, I randomly opened the Bible to this passage: "with the soles of my feet I have dried up all the streams of Egypt."

THE RISE OF THE
ANTI-CHRIST

THE 2023 GRAMMY AWARDS SPONSORED BY PFIZER WHO HAS MADE
BILLIONS FROM THE PLANNEDEMIC SAW THE VERY SATANIC
PERFORMANCE BY NON-BINARY ARTIST SAM SMITH WHO WORE
DEVILISH HORNS AS HE SANG "UNHOLY."

Apocalypse

WHILE WE STILL HAVE THE ILLUSION OF FREE SPEECH, MANY VIDEOS HAVE APPEARED ACROSS SOCIAL MEDIA PLATFORMS PERTAINING TO THE TIMING OF AN APOCALYPSE, REVELATIONS, THE RAPTURE AND RISE OF THE ANTI-CHRIST.

Any individual inviting Satan into the fold brings endless amounts of suffering. These entities come with the End Times, furthering my resolve of the current status in the world.

Financial status, or fame, has somehow come to dictate the tyrannical dictatorship of the world's population. The main goal is separating us from the Kingdom of Heaven. The images in this chapter show the appearance of fallen angels or demonic entities being driven toward the light.

My prayers since writing '*The New Wine*' have included the higher Angels drive these entities back to a heaven away from any influence in human affairs. I can tell you the occult and black magic, sorcery, witchcraft, and outright Satanism will bring these things into our dimensions.

Active scientific experiments at C.E.R.N. with particle colliders will hasten this cross-dimensional penetration of our world and everything that comes with it. In fact, everything I believe is currently anti-Christ driven: a senseless war in Ukraine, private billionaires dictating medical and political policy, rampant drug trade, sex trafficking, demonic rituals, and films or music recordings glorifying demons, a digitized banking system, trans-humanism or the merging of technology with human biology, and "rigged" political elections. Mr. Musk for example has openly divulged his plan to implant a microchip into our brains. Not one of these things is the will of Our Father in Heaven for his children. We have strength in numbers, and it is up to us to unite as one body and stand up against evil tyrannical control.

A highly blasphemous and Anti-Christ photo of singer Demi Lovato on a bed shaped as a cross in S&M bondage is clearly satanic and Anti-Christian. I found this ironic as she, like Katy Perry, began her career as a Christian.

A photo of Elon Musk wearing a clearly satanic suit of armor with a baphomet skull and upside down cross to a Halloween party clearly would suggest an Anti-Christ viewpoint towards the world.

Photo: More demonic energies being driven out by higher order angels of light. You can clearly see how angry their faces are for they love control in this world.

Photo: More demonic energies being driven out by higher order angels of light. You can clearly see how angry their faces are for they love control in this world.

Photo: More demonic energies being driven out by higher order angels of light. You can clearly see how angry their faces are, for they love control in this world. What is interesting about the photos on the top row is they came right after a "random" opening of the Bible to a passage on the "fall of Lucifer."

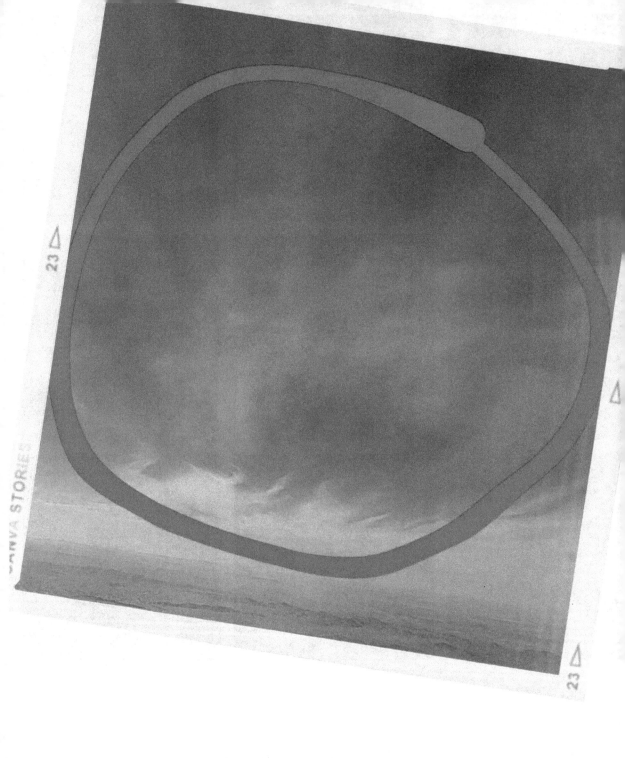

Photo: More demonic energies being driven out by higher order angels of light. You can clearly see how angry their faces are for they love control in this world. What is interesting about the photos on the top row is they came right after a "random" opening of the Bible to a passage on the "fall of Lucifer."

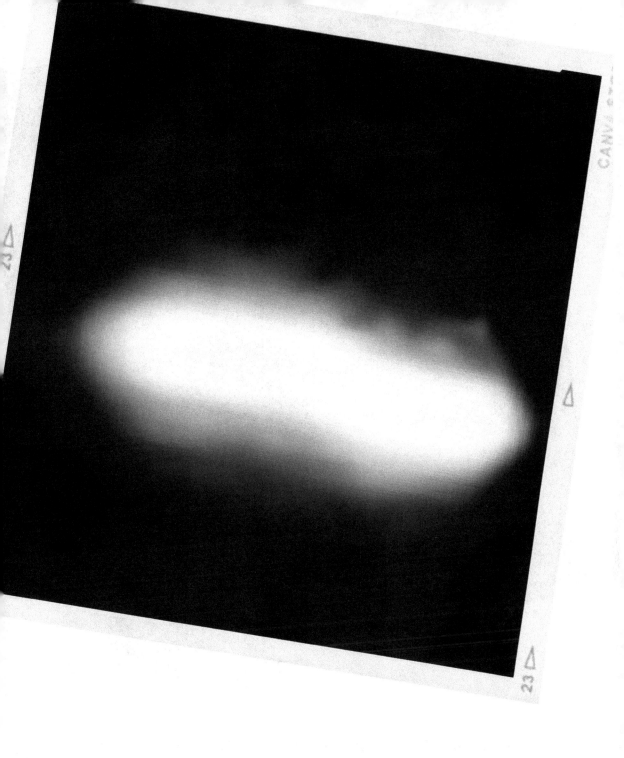

Photo: An incredible face and light above my roof on November 18th, 2022.

Photo: On November 22nd, 2022 this angry-looking demonic face with horns appeared at sunset in central Arizona. I showed the image to someone I had been talking with who felt that someone close to them was possessed and she said this is what she saw in this individual. It is my belief this is Satan/Lucifer/Hillel Ben Shachar/Red Dragon/Devil/Memnoch/Baphomet. As you can see our work is not quite finished.

Key of Believe

The only way to defeat the enemy is with the key of believe.

Believe in yourself, your fellow man or woman, and God to win this battle. If we all stand in unity against the very things that threaten our survival, he cannot win. There is no host for him to consume.

C IS FOR
CAREY

ANOTHER LOVELY MEMORY AND PHOTOGRAPH OF CAREY WHO CAME
TO ME FROM THE OTHER KINGDOM IN THE FALL OF 2022 WITH MANY
MESSAGES FOR HER FAMILY.

Connections

The next story is one of the most beautiful afterlife interactions of my life. While working in a hospital in Phoenix, Arizona, a staff member named Lindsay and I discussed life, death, afterlife and reincarnation. The conversation led to my books. She wanted to know more about my spiritual experiences.

Later Lindsay sent me a photo of her mom named Carey. The encounter was unexpected, since she was looking for someone who could contact her mother in the other Kingdom. We agreed I would try to reach out.

My drive home from work that day left me amazed again. Before even praying about the connection, Carey found me driving home. The following images are examples of the messages sent from heaven.

After Carey sent me some information about her mom only, she would know, the messages appeared almost immediately. As an example, I saw images of a school Carey worked at years ago. Then a red plaid flannel shirt, she said her father wore regularly.

She replied, "I can be the wind."

"Thank you, my gift continually gets more honed."

"Matthew, this is amazing, because I have had some recent experiences where I felt my mom's spirit in the wind."

Lindsay continued to show me images, including a young boy, who ended up being her 8-year-old son. After which, Carey showed me chocolate bars, because Lindsay said due to a medical condition, she could not eat it anymore.

It did not stop there, Carey showed me what looked like Pro Wrestling images, and Lindsay verified her brothers' attended matches. Then I saw an amusement park with roller coasters. Lindsay said their family loved Universal Studios.

Photo: On November 30th, 2022 another huge angel with a large "C" appeared above my home in Arizona. Carey is always near us with her new wings.

Photo: A beautiful photograph of Carey who came to me from the other kingdom in the Fall of 2022 with many messages for her family.

Photo: Another amazing heart and huge angels appear following spiritual communication with a woman named Carey who was coming through for her daughter Lindsay and her grandson.

Photo: Another awesome family photograph of Carey and her family on one of the many trips to Universal in Orlando. Carey showed me she would be on the roller coaster next to her daughter now and forever.

Photo: Amazing huge "C's" appear after being contacted by a friend's mother named Carey following her passing. Carey gave me many messages for her daughter Lindsay that only she would know.

Photo: Carey's father wore a red plaid flannel shirt and this was one of the first images she gave me in my mind's eye to let her daughter know we were communicating from beyond this realm.

Photo: More "C's" appear following contact with a woman named Carey whose daughter Lindsay had been trying to reach her in the spirit realm. Some of these images are simply stunning.

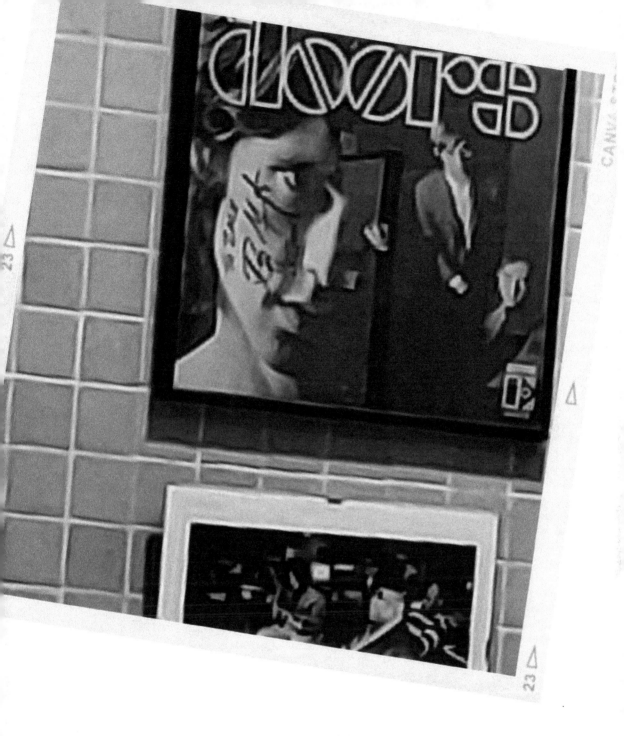

Photo: After Lindsay and her family took their annual trip to Universal Studios Lindsay sent this image with an text that said: "got on my mom's favorite roller coaster and there was an open seat right next to me like you said there would be, and then we went to breakfast and you were staring right at me."

'Key of Believe'

Carey's story is amazing, especially how she came through before
any prayers in church. She had spot on messages only her
daughter would understand, including the empty seat on the
roller coaster ride.

However, the most amazing message came when she informed me
of waiting after the ride to validate who I am and why I am ... so I
live for life, *'In The Key Of Believe'*.

THE
TRINITY

ON JANUARY 19TH, 2023 THIS ODD LOOKING SAUCER AND ROSE
SHAPED CLOUD APPEARED ABOVE TURKEY.ON MONDAY, FEBRUARY
6TH, 2023 A MASSIVE 7.8 EARTHQUAKE STRUCK TURKEY KILLING
THOUSANDS. I DO NOT BELIEVE THESE EVENTS TO BE UNRELATED
AND FURTHER PROVE WE ARE IN REVELATIONS.

Show Us the Way

As the world teeters on WW III, or the possibility of nuclear Armageddon, the natural disasters continue at a frequency seemingly unprecedented, yet apparitions of 'The Woman Clothed in the Sun" shine bright in the skies above. In my first book 'The New Wine' after witnessing the Son of Jesus and Holy Spirit on many occasions in 2017, I firmly believe it's time to restore the key of believe.

Some of the photographs in this chapter show clearly the entities from Heaven are trying to guide our path to redemption, if we choose to listen.

If you look at 2022, we saw the "blizzard of the century" that killed dozens of people. In early 2023, a massive "bomb cyclone" brought storms and flooding to large swaths of California. On November 20th, 2022, another volcanic explosion occurred in Russia. These instances in my opinion are not coincidence, as the world plummets into chaos. Recent reports also show China will at some point invade Twain.

Amongst societal beliefs, many are veering to the idea that evil will continue to force endless wars, providing greed to overcome Christian values. A belief system that has been indoctrinated into society for many decades, trying to convince people Satan is the all-mighty overlord. However, nothing could be further from the truth. 'In The Key Of Believe', I challenge the notion.

The average person does not want war, it's again being forced down our throats by a small minority of elites trying to convince the large majority of false evidence. As I continue to write, the key of believe, the world can change, but we must come together as ONE. Only then can we change the world.

The world's largest volcano, Mauna Loa in Hawaii, erupts on November 28th, 2022 in a wing shape formation of lava.

Photo: More incredible images of both Jesus Christ, St. Mary, and the Holy Spirit Paraclete as well as the face of The Father and an Angel of the Lord in 2022 as the world teeters on the brink of world war III.

Photo: Incredible miraculous appearances of St. Mary and The Son Jesus (top left) as well as an unexplained water stain next to St. Germaine Catholic Church in Prescott Valley, Arizona in 2022. You can even see a small heart inside the "water angel" that is deliberate and beautiful. In the bottom right FRAME, you can see Mother Mary riding a heart shaped cloud.

Photo: More incredible images of Our Mother Mary appearing with powerful Angels and the amazing water angel apparition near St. Germain Catholic Church in Prescott Valley, Arizona in 2022 as the world nears a dangerous time in its history.

Photo: The morning of November 28th, 2022 this amazing orange angelic like wing appeared above a local church right as the world's largest volcano Mauna Loa in Hawaii also erupted in a wing like shape.

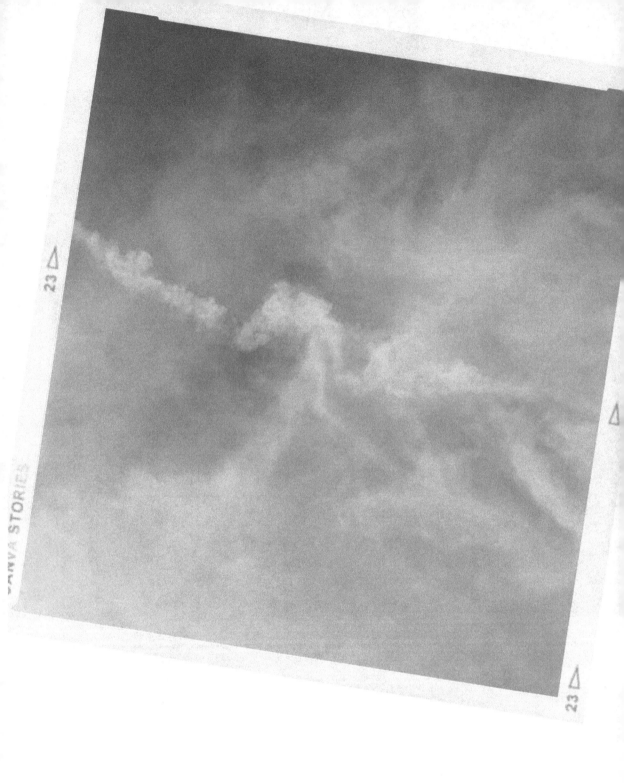

Photo: On November 28th, 2022 this incredible unicorn shaped cloud appeared above Phoenix, Arizona next to a rainbow colored cloud.

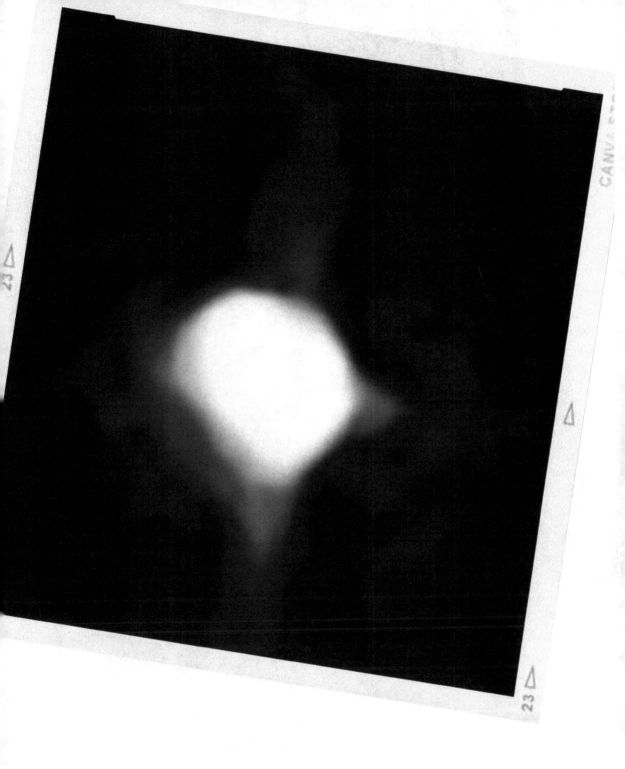

Photo: On November 20th, 2022 I took a photo of this "star" in the skies above our home and blew it up. You can clearly see a figure seeming to ride the star. This is very apocalyptic looking.

Photo: A Russian volcano explodes on November 20th, 2022 as the Russian invasion of the Ukraine continues bringing the world closer to nuclear war. There is no greater time in history to use the key of believe to make the world understand we cannot continue on this course.

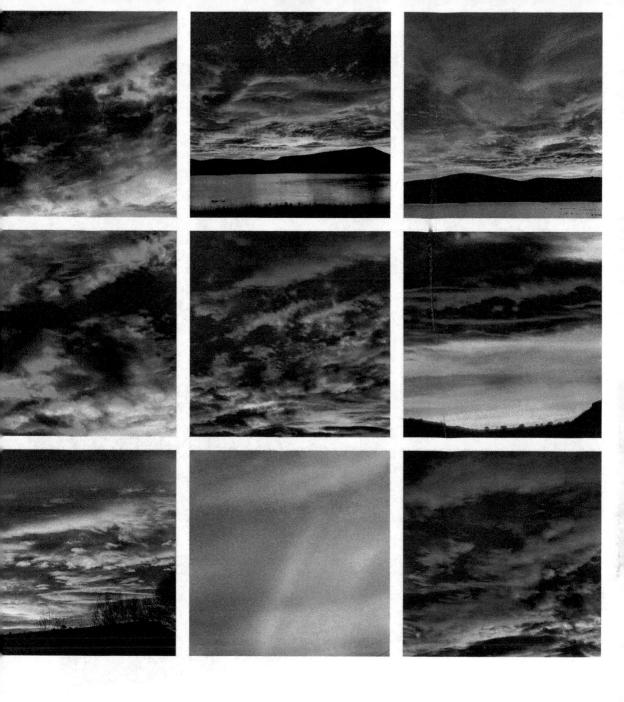

Photo: The morning of December 27th, 2022 saw one of the most amazing sunrises I've ever personally witnessed. This came after a morning Rosary for world peace and for the world to turn away from wars and greed, and for the truth behind the plannedemic to be exposed. I see a cross top left, a huge wing middle top row and multiple demonic faces being exorcised from the earth.

Photo: In yet another apocalyptic scene a volcano in Guatemala erupted on December 11th, 2022.

Photo: This view of Mauna Loa volcano eruption on November 29th, 2022 shows what appears to be an angel bearing a cross next to a "J" for Jesus. I believe the world is being shown a greater power on earth in an effort to bring peace and equality to the world.

CANVA STORIES

23

23

Photo: On November 29th, 2022 as Mauna Loa continues to erupt in Hawaii two very demonic looking faces appear in the eruption.

Photo: An amazing shot of Mauna Loa erupting in Hawaii and two very odd looking faces to the top right of the frame.

Photo: Another serious volcanic eruption of the Stromboli Volcano in Italy also occurred on December 4th, 2022 as more volcanoes erupt across the planet as further confirmation of apocalyptic wrath.

Photo: On December 10th, 2022 another volcano erupted in Chile high into the atmosphere evoking this very apocalyptic image.

Photo: On Sunday, December 4th, 2022 Mount Semeru in Indonesia erupted on Java Island. This is further proof we are in the Book of Revelations.

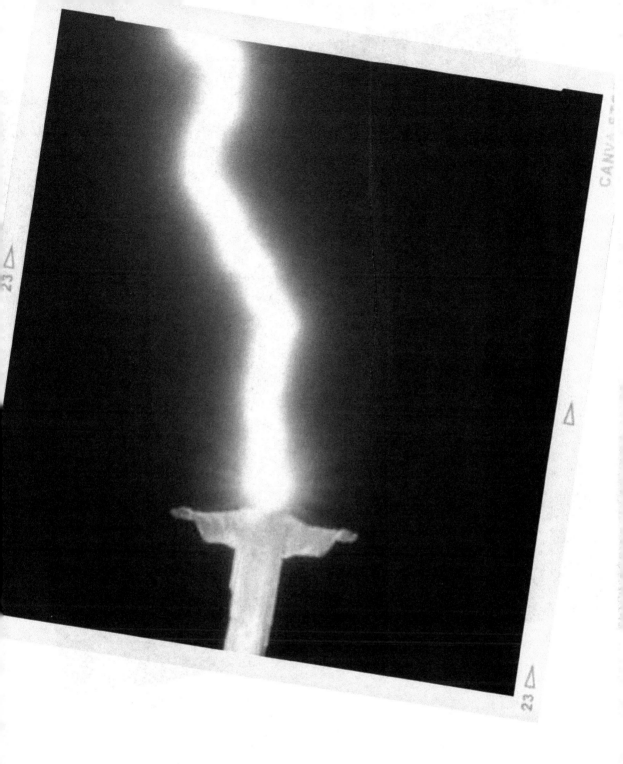

Photo: In an incredibly apocalyptic image, a lightning bolt struck the top of the head of the Christ the Redeemer statue in Brazil on Friday, February 10th, 2023 causing many Christians worldwide to proclaim this is a clear message from God to repent and accept his Son Jesus Christ. I fully agree with this assertion.

STORIES 23 23

Photo: In mid February this amazing blood crescent moon appeared above the Sea of Galilee while many had apocalyptic and rapturous dreams at the same time. This is further proof we are in End Times.

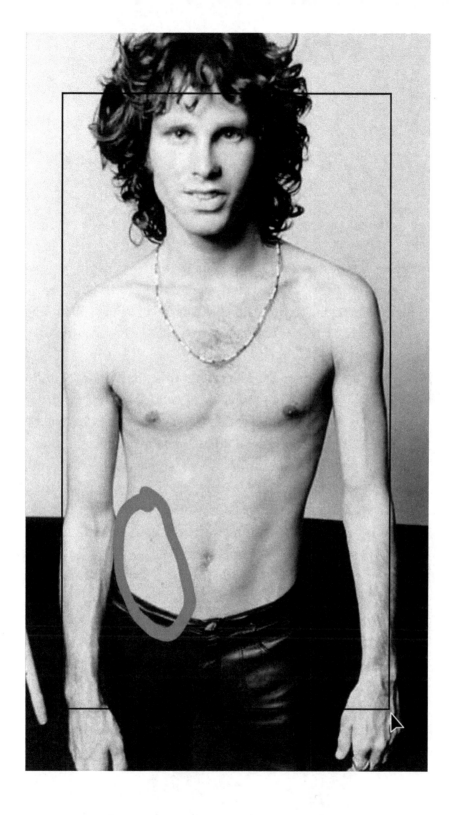

Photo: James Douglas Morrison circa 1960's as part of The Doors musical group. You can clearly see the three "belt" stars of Orion on his right stomach. As I mentioned in previous BOOKS, I am Jim's reincarnation and conjoined "Son" spirit, the left and right jaws of God and Saint Mary.

Key of Believe

In the last section of 'The Trinity', a parallel relationship between myself and half-brother, previous incarnation spirit host James Douglas Morrison, was described as the 'devil' by the spiritually blind. On the other hand, some have used the description of mystical prophets, truth 'seers' so to speak.

Some time ago, I came across a photograph of James in the mid-60s, while part of The Doors. On the right side of the stomach are three moles, which symbolizes 'belt' stars of the Orion Nebula.

Both are from 'An' or 'Eden/Heaven' resides.

After viewing this photograph, it appeared I also have the same mole pattern. The discovery is further proof, I am not only the reincarnation of James Douglas Morrison, but also the 'Son', which has now been 'stacked', meaning we are conjoined eternally, one body, one spirit, one soul.

The images of James provide evidence we/us stand for equality of mankind, are against wars, greed, idolatry, Satanism, murder, assaults, mistreatment of animals, and godlessness.

As Jim prayed in "An American Prayer" and I pray now, the world must recognize change before it is too late. Some events could make the planet truly inhabitable.

The time for prayer has come. We must look for ways to find peace among the population and reject tyranny.

ME AND JULIO DOWN BY
THE SCHOOLYARD

VIVIAN AND JULIO PRIOR TO JULIO'S UNTIMELY PASSING FROM COVID. THEY ARE A HAPPY AND ETERNALLY IN LOVE COUPLE WHOSE LOVE KNOWS NO BOUNDARIES.

Soulmates

As you will read in the next story, soulmates exist in this realm and the other Kingdom. In August 2022, a friend referred Vivian to me. Her husband Julio passed away due to COVID.

Vivian rightly so, was devastated. She asked me if I could contact Julio in the spirit world, and make sure he was okay. We discussed my process and how I would contact him. Within minutes of ending our call, enormous 'J's' appeared in the sky. The response amazed me.

Later that day, I have a vision of Julio on a beach wearing a straw hat. Vivian immediately forwarded a photo of Julio on the beach wearing the same hat in my vision. She told me they had gone on a cruise before his passing.

The 'J's' kept coming for days, Julio was now with his father in heaven. Then, he asked me to tell Vivian they would be together again one day, promise.

Photo: Julio Almuina on a cruise wearing the same straw hat he showed me in a vision. His arms are out as if saying "welcome to my Heaven." Julio's untimely passing from COVID was not the end of his life in Christ.

Photo: Enormous "J's" appear in the skies above Arizona in August of 2022 following spiritual contact with Julio Almuina. What Was amazing was a double rainbow also formed which was significant as Julio was coming from Heaven with his father also named Julio.

Photo: Enormous "J's" appear in the skies above Arizona in August of 2022 following spiritual contact with Julio Almuina. You can clearly see the huge angels that brought Julio back to earth as well as numerous hearts in the skies.

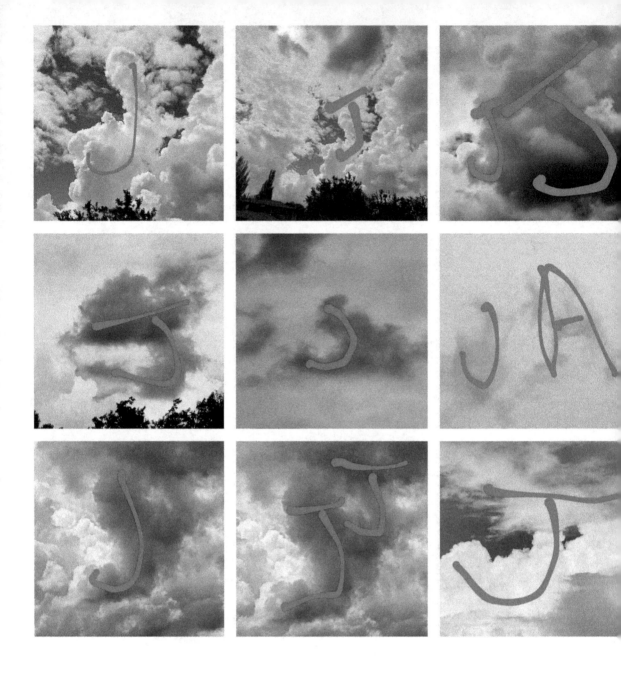

Photo: Enormous "J's" appears in the skies above Arizona in August of 2022 following spiritual contact with Julio. One of the frames shows his full initials, "J.A.."

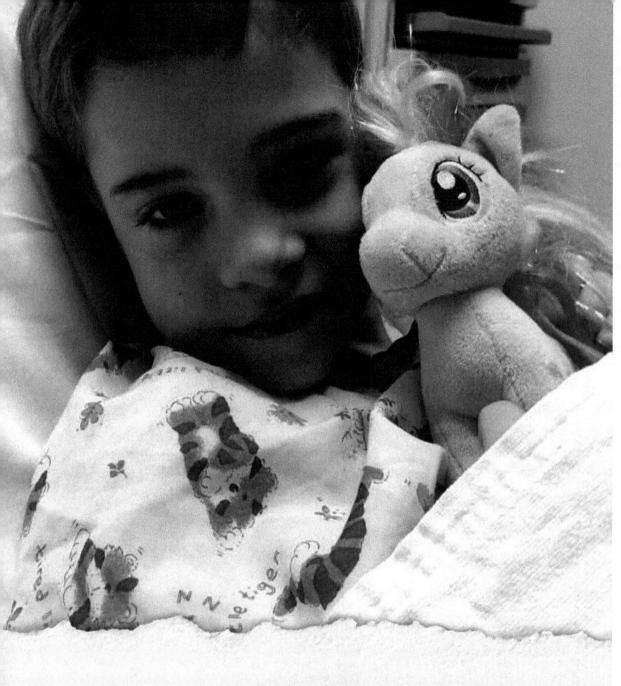

TRENTON'S
ANGEL

YOUNG PAXTON ELKINS AS HE COURAGEOUSLY BATTLED
TERMINAL BRAIN CANCER IN 2017.

"Many of my readers will remember the story of young Paxton
Elkins from my first three books in the *New Wine* book series"

Miracles

On June 8th, 2023, when working near Tucson, Arizona at the home healthcare company, an incredible angel appeared, forming a 'P' and a 'T' in the skies with a rainbow halo. Immediately, thought of Paxton.

I sent the image to Paxton's mother Krista in Indiana, and she asked when the photo was taken. As it turned out, unbeknown to me, Paxton's older brother Trenton was in a serious car accident but walked away relatively unscathed. In speaking with Krista, we both agreed that Paxton played a role in saving his brother's life that day.

photo: The SUV that Trenton Elkins walked away from after a roll over accident in Indiana on June 8th, 2023.

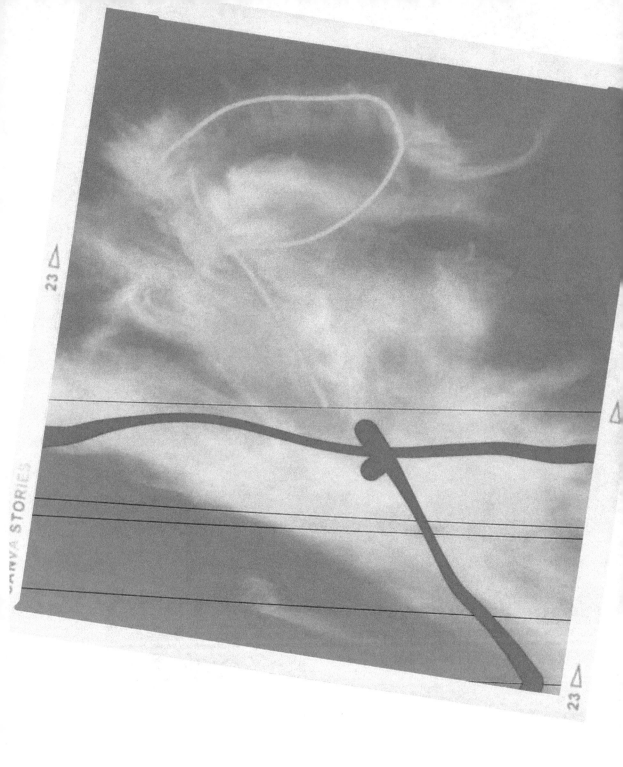

Photo: The incredible rainbow colored angel that formed a "P" and "T" for Paxton and Trenton on June 8th, 2023 above Tucson, Arizona where I was working. This is no doubt a sign from Heaven that Paxton was watching over his brother Trenton that day following a serious auto accident.

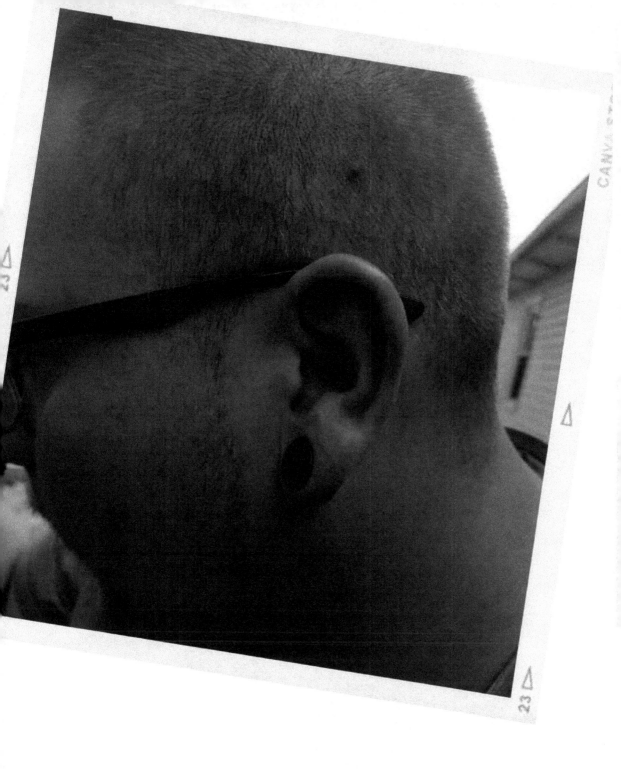

Photo: Trenton Elkins with only minor injuries after a roll over auto accident in Indiana on June 8th, 2023.

'Key of Believe'

Young Paxton Elkins story blessed my first book, 'T*he New Wine.*'
In the book I explained the two keys given by Jesus to St. Peter. In
all my research, no one has discussed the symbolism behind the
keys: 'be love' and 'believe.'

There is no doubt that Paxton was able to save his brother Trenton
with that very key, the key of believe.

PIGTAILS AND THE
RADIO FLYER

MY GOOD FRIEND LIANE AS A CHILD WAS DRESSED IN PIG TAILS BY HER MOTHER ELAINE WHICH WAS SHOWN TO ME IN A VISION AFTER MANY E'S APPEARED IN THE SKIES.

Eternally

The continued miracles presented right before my eyes each day are incredible. A friend of mine, Liane, who works at the clubhouse in our subdivision, made a request one day after a conversation about my books. She asked me to contact a woman named Elaine.

In this instance, I was given no information about the identity of this person but had a notion it might be her mother. A day later, after my usual Rosary, numerous messages showed me a red flyer wagon, a young girl with amber hair in pigtails. Plus, the usual 'Es' in the skies.

Upon our next conversation, Liane informed me her mom always did her hair in pigtails. One of the final memories she had of her mother was eating ice cream in the red wagon.

The main message of our encounter was to let the world know - death is not the end. Our memories live eternally with our loved ones.

Photo: The red radio flyer wagon was the first image received from a woman named Elaine for her daughter Liane.

Photo: One of the last photos of Liane with her mother Elaine who visited me psychically and showed me this moment with them grabbing ice cream prior to her passing to the other kingdom.

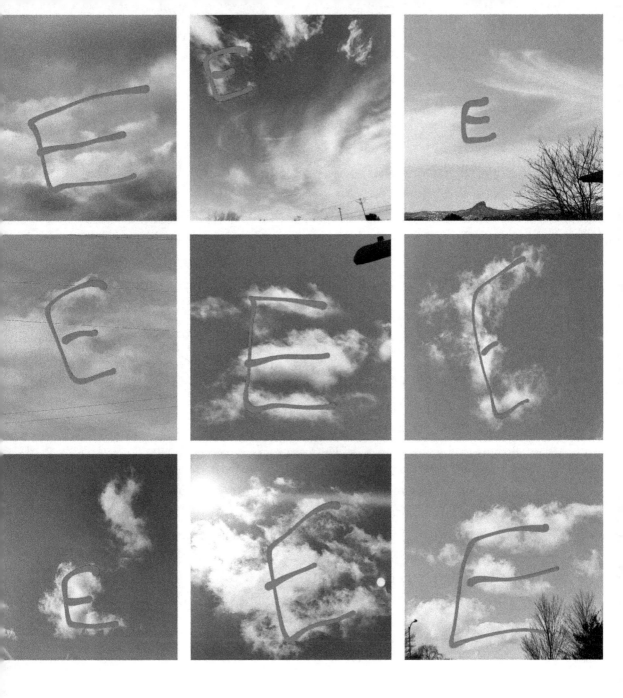

Photo: Numerous "E's" from Elaine appeared as she visited us in spirit in January 2023 with many messages for her daughter Liane from the other kingdom.

'Key of Believe'

Once again, I pray my readers will see with 'the key of believe', we can still live in eternal memory with our loved ones, who are never far from us even in 'death.'

Anyone who yearns to open their third eye will receive messages from the other Kingdom Spirit Realm. It is in that world: the truth is held, why we are here on earth, and what truly comes after life on this plane.

J.C.'S
WOLF

A BEAUTIFUL PHOTO OF J.C. THROWING HIS SON IN THE AIR ON THE BEACH LIVING LIFE FREE OF HIS "WOLF" LUPUS DISEASE THAT NO LONGER ATTACKS HIS BODY.

Believe

A dear friend recently asked me to pray for her cousin J.C., who had been diagnosed with Lupus in 2022.

Lupus is the Latin word for 'wolf' after a thirteenth-century physician described erosive facial features from Lupus as resembling a wolf's bite.

After my prayers for J.C. and asking the angels to heal his Lupus, these amazing images appeared soon after. You can clearly see many of his initials in the skies, as well as hearts, pyramid portals, rainbow, and angel wings.

Photo: Incredible "J" and "C" initials appear in the skies above Arizona along with a rainbow and pyramid portal signaling the angels heard prayers for J.C.'s lupus.

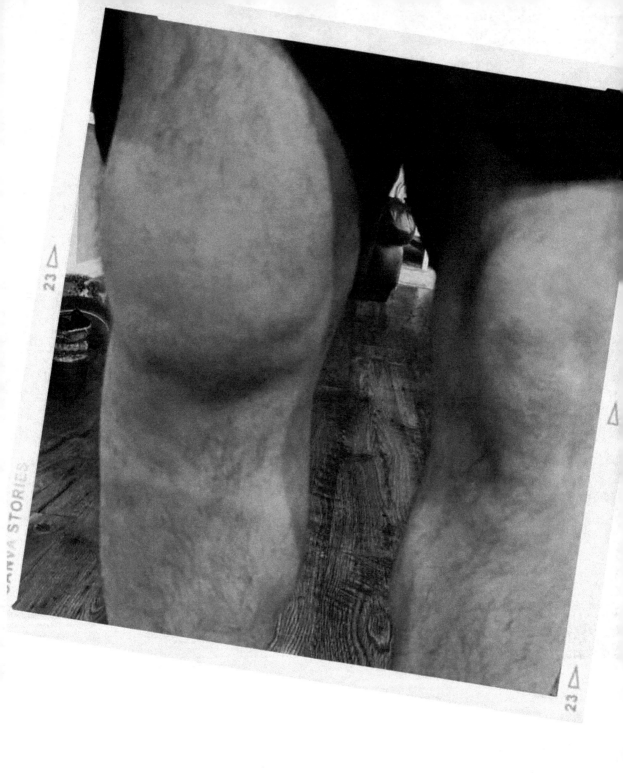

Photo: This unbelievable photo from July 2022 shows a severely inflamed right leg of J.C. Lupus is an autoimmune disease where the body attacks itself causing chronic painful inflammation. J.C. said, "this is the last flare up he had before a miraculous healing and he is not on any medication anymore."

Photo: Amazing "Cs" and "Js" appear above central Arizona following prayers for J.C. to be healed of lupus.

Photo: An extraordinary photo of huge "J.C." initials and a huge angel "blowing out" the wolf lupus from J.C.'s body in 2022 following prayers for angelic miraculous healing.

Key of Believe

Yet, another amazing miracle occurred after the next visit to J.C.'s rheumatologist, and extensive testing; no Lupus present in the body.

"The results were mind blowing Matthew. I cannot believe someone I have never met, who could make my initials appear in the skies and my test results show me disease free. Thanks Matt."

Once again, we defeated 'disease' with the key of believe.

A RED CAR AND
A CUTTY

THE IMAGE IS THE EXACT TYPE OF "CUTTY SHIP" I SAW IN MY
PSYCHIC VISION. IT LED TO THE KILLER OF TWO YOUNG TEENS IN
INDIANA. THIS ITEM IS SOLD IN CVS PHARMACIES WHERE THE
KILLER WORKED IN 2017.

Reveal

In '*The New Wine*" is a story about two brutal murders in states near Michigan. At the time, my wife and I lived not far away. After seeing the local news story, I prayed about Jayme Closs's whereabouts. She was 13 and kidnapped at gunpoint after witnessing her parents murdered in front of her by an unknown suspect.

Our prayers revealed some specific messages — a log cabin in the woods, a red car or SUV, a business called 'Joe's Repair Shop' and a county fair.

After finding out a county fair was held in their hometown, and in fact, the town had a 'Joe's Repair Shop,' I called the FBI. Thankfully, an agent followed up the next day. As the days passed, the case went viral. Jayme Closs bravely escaped her abductor and was found alive.

She was also, in fact, held in a cabin in the woods. Recently, I found a photo online of her abductor's vehicle, which can be seen below.

The next high-profile case involved the brazen murder of teens Abigail Williams and Liberty German in Delphi, Indiana 2017. The case actually affected my wife deeply as I used to hike in the same area where the girls were murdered.

After a few days of praying, some clear messages came through and I called law enforcement. The tip included an image of a Cutty Ship, like an old sailing vessel. It was either on a shelf or definitely important. After more than five years, Richard Mattew Allen was finally arrested.

What I found quite interesting is the clue of a "cutty ship" I had given authorities is an image found on products inside a local CVS where Mr. Allen had worked for many years.

STORIES

23

VIDEO FROM JAYME CLOSS KIDNAPP

23

Photo: The red car of suspect and confessed killer and kidnapper Jake Patterson after his arrest and conviction. I was accurate in terms of the color and size of the vehicle in my psychic vision I gave to the authorities.

Photo: Old Spice deodorant which also carries a "cutty ship" image as its brand as found on local CVS pharmacies such as the one where a killer of two young teens in Indiana worked. My psychic vision of a cutty ship being important to the case was accurate.

Photo: Confessed killer and kidnapper Jake Patterson in court before being sentenced to life for the Jayme Closs case in Wisconsin.

'Key of Believe'

The horrific evidence compiled on this case tried to force doubt, but I had faith in my vision. Thank God, my phone tip ended in an arrest of the man convicted of these inconceivable crimes against children. Just more proof the key of believe is the answer to living by faith.

COPD

Chronic Obstructive Pulmonary Disease

B'S

ANGEL LUNGS

INCREDIBLE ANGELS AND CLEAR LUNGS AND FIERY SUNSETS
FOLLOWING PRAYERS FOR A CLOSE RELATIVE

Angels

In March 2022, a close friend called about their recent medial diagnosis. After experiencing shortness of breath, and mild dizziness, they went for a consult. The test results showed moderate COPD. I immediately offered to pray for healing.
Enormous angels appeared, even before St. Patrick's Day, with a rainbow-colored head.

Then continued with numerous pairs of 'lungs', along with his initials "B." In the preceding weeks, amazing angels appeared with fiery sunsets and more "B" initials, and even pairs of lungs as angel wings, but clear of disease.

Photo: More amazing angels, initial "B" and fiery sunsets from March and April 2022 after prayers for a relative with the initial "B" with a lung disease diagnosis. The most impressive ones on this page are the rainbow colored head of an angel on St. Patrick's Day and also a huge diving Holy Spirit Paraclete.

Photos: initial "B" to heal them of moderate lung disease all appeared above central Arizona in March and April 2022.

'Key of Believe'

Shortly after the messages from angels, a phone call revealed a clean bill of health. A recent appointment for testing showed no moderate COPD or emphysema. Not only that, but this person does not need an inhaler or oxygen tank.
To this date, this diagnosis shows no degeneration in the lungs. So, could this be considered a miracle from heaven? I know what my answer is ...

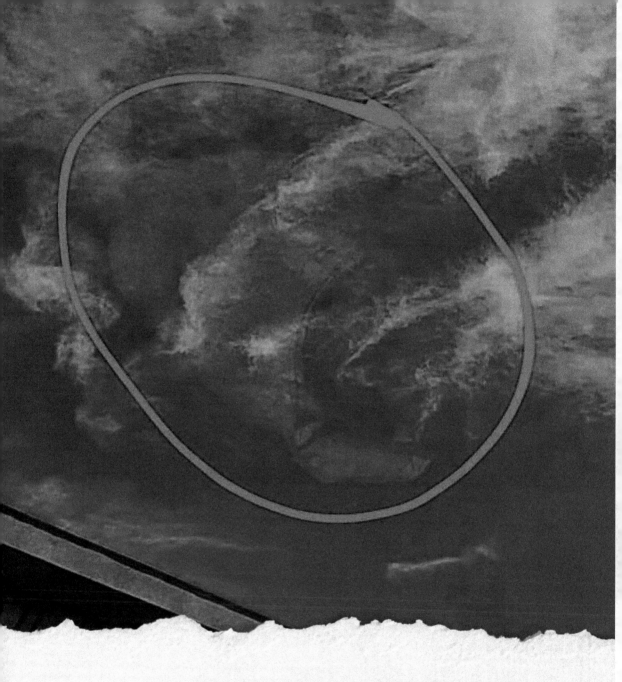

THE GHOST OF
OCEAN'S GATE

MISSING SUBMARINE NAMED "OCEAN'S GATE"

Relevance

On Monday, June 19th, 2023, while in Phoenix, Arizona calling on local hospitals I photographed one of the most paranormal apparitions I've ever taken that clearly seemed to bear relevance to the worldwide news of a missing submarine named "Ocean's Gate" that disappeared from communication the previous day. What is amazing about the photograph below is it appears to show a large angelic figure with wings and face and horns "carrying" what clearly appears to be a submarine-shaped object in the sky. It is clear this was not a "reflection" from my car.

The apparition is yet again more proof that angels follow us even in the most difficult and tragic of times."

hello!

Matthew Douglas Pinard is the author of *The New Wine* series. He was born and raised in southeastern Michigan and has a bachelor's degree in psychology from the University of Michigan and a master's degree in military history from Louisiana State University. Matthew is also a former US Army JAG legal specialist. He and his wife Carol Rose are recent transplants from west Michigan and now live in beautiful Prescott Valley, Arizona, with their two dogs Reese, a chocolate Lab, and Cleetus, a Redbone Coonhound. Matthew is a ranked Shihan (sixth degree) in Hakko Den shin Ryu Japanese Jujutsu and enjoys hiking, communing with the other side, praying for world peace, and photographing archangels in his spare time.

COPYRIGHT © 2023 MATTHEW DOUGLAS PINARD

OTHER BOOKS BY AUTHOR

matthewpinardauthor.com

Follow Me:
- Goodreads
- Author Central

Screenplay Awards
Matthew Douglas Pinard

Official Selection

Bloodstained Indie Film Festival

StoryPros Awards Screenplay Contest

Military Script Showcase

L.A. Neo Noir Novel Film & Script Festival

True Story International Film Festival

Reel Heart International Film Festival

Hollywood Boulevard International Film Festival

Independent Talents International Film Festival

Fort Worth Indie Film Showcase

California Independent Film Festival

San Pedro International Film Festival,

Southeastern International Film Festival

Louisiana International Film Festival

Official Selection

First Ten Pages Script Contest
Atlanta Comedy Film Festival
Georgia Shorts Film Festival
Official Finalist
Las Vegas International Film and Screenwriting Contest, Honorable Mention
Depth of Field International Film Festival, Award Winner
Beverly Hills International Film Festival, Silver Winner
Queen Palm International Film Festival, Award Winner
Colorado International Film Festival, Quarter-Finalist
Chicago Screenplay Awards, Quarter-Finalist
NYC International Screenplay Awards, Quarter-Finalist
Atlanta Screenplay Awards, Semi-Finalist
Cordillera International Film Festival, Semi-Finalist
Fade In Awards, Finalist
Breaking Walls Thriller Screenplay Award Winner
Vegas Movie Awards,
The Santa Barbara International Screenplay Awards, Finalist
Miami Screen Play Awards, Quarter-Finalist

Printed in the USA
CPSIA information can be obtained
at www.ICGtesting.com
LVHW080050260823
756141LV00002B/40